MALDEN — Old & New
REV

G000254739

Dedicated to Mrs Violet Jay (nee Lavender)
— the original collector of these postcards

Stephen H. Day

ACKNOWLEDGEMENTS

Most of the postcards used in this book are from the collection of
Margaret Hurley
a former resident of New Malden, now living in Lancaster.
They were made available for the author's use by her great generosity.

———————

The author also wishes to thank several local Senior Citizens for their
memories and help; those who kindly made other material available
either for reproduction or to assist research, together with Organisations etc.
that gave access for modern photographs:

Eileen Abbott   Gwen and Peter Avis   Ruth Hicks

Kingsmeadow Stadium   Kingston Heritage Centre

Les Kirkin

London Fire Brigade
Assistant Divisional Officer Stevens and
White Watch of New Malden Fire Station

Malden Wanderer's Cricket Club

Yvonne Matts

Remington Consumer Products Ltd. Apex Tower

June Sampson   The Surrey Comet

Mr and Miss Tolley

and very special thanks to TONY DURRANT of THE MARINE PRESS

First published and © 1991 by
Marine Day Publishers
64 Cotterill Road, Surbiton KT6 7UN
Surrey.
Tel: 081 399 7625

All rights reserved. No part of this publication may be reproduced, stored in a retrieval system,
or transmitted in any form without permission of the publisher.

ISBN 0 9516076 1 8 MALDEN — Old & New REVISITED: A Second Pictorial History (pbk)

Printed and bound for The Marine Press Ltd.
by Alderson Brothers Printers Ltd., Hersham, Surrey.

CONTENTS

INTRODUCTION

The publication in July 1990 of *Malden — Old & New* was the culmination of three years spare-time work and the result of an enthusiasm for local history from old picture postcards, rather than any attempt to claims of writer or historian. The compilation and presentation of relevant, interesting material and the design and layout of the finished book were just as important to me as historical accuracy — something for which admittedly, I relied heavily upon other people's work. What was to have been a 'one-off' project completed at my leisure, then became a challenge to complete a second book.

This came about when the phone rang after Christmas, and Margaret Hurley introduced herself as an ex-resident of The Village, and owner of a copy of *the book*. 'Could we meet sometime, as she also had a collection of New Malden cards which might be of interest?' [I have *yet* to meet Margaret, and look forward to it]. The cards were strictly 'not for sale' as they had the sentimental value of having been passed on to her through her mother, from the original collector, Mrs Violet Jay. Mrs Jay (nee Lavender) was a close neighbour when Margaret was a girl living at *Rose Cottages*, Grafton Road [now the site of Tregarron Gardens]. She and husband Jim had no children of their own, and Margaret and her brother were therefore treated like grand-children. Margaret always enjoyed looking through Violet's picture postcards and because of this interest, subsequently became the owner of the collection when she died in 1981.

Margaret was just on her way home to Lancaster when she made that phone call to me, but kindly offered to send a list of some sixty postcard subjects by post. When these arrived a few days later I could tell without seeing the actual cards, that here was a collection of rare, 'dated event' cards which deserved a wider audience. I wrote back suggesting that between us, we had the makings of a second, very different pictorial history. Living far away, and with the responsibility of a young family would have made this very difficult for Margaret. Instead, she very generously offered the exclusive opportunity of this second book to me, and arranged for the collection of the postcards from her parent's home in Norbiton.

I hope that in the relatively short space of time since then, I have made the best possible use of her postcards, a few of my own, together with the principal sources of reference, *The Surrey Comet* — and the memories of several local Senior Citizens, who have related the kind of information unavailable in newspapers, street directories, maps or guide books.

In the Introduction to *'Malden — Old & New'*, I used an appropriate quotation from the book *Half a Century of Kingston History* written over one hundred years ago by F.S. Merryweather — a founding father of New Malden. Having now completed an unexpected, second pictorial history by revisiting where possible, the scenes of these postcards in order to take *more* up-to-date photographs, I can think of only one apt saying — "History repeats itself".

I hope you enjoy looking through these pages as much as I enjoyed compiling them.

Stephen Day

Foreword

It is a great compliment to be asked to write a foreword, but one that I usually decline. The reason is that the books concerned do not adequately fill what is surely the role of any local history work worth publishing, namely to inform as well as to entertain.

Plenty set out to do the latter. It is, after all, very good for quick sales. Far fewer achieve the former, which involves careful research and a refusal to blur fact with unsubstantiated myth simply to make a more colourful story.

Stephen Day's first book was, in my view, a little masterpiece of its kind. So is his second.

Like the first, it is essentially a picture book, and he allows the cameras — his own and those of past observers — to provide the main narrative. But he also provides invaluable background information in the form of well chosen captions.

These look deceptively short and simple. In fact, they represent long hours of research, and his meticulous quoting of all his sources will be a boon to those who, appetites whetted by this volume, are eager to learn more.

Be warned, though. These photographs are not only fascinating. Some also evoke an aching nostalgia for a lost past; a prickle of envy for those who lived in it, and experienced pleasures (as well as hardships, no doubt) that we shall never know; and, above all, a recurring rage and sadness that we have so despoiled a landscape that once had so much character and charm.

Look at page 21. Or, for a far more jolting example, at page 28. This is what is popularly known as "progress"!

June Sampson

Features Editor, 'Surrey Comet'

Original Publishers of the Postcards — some notes and dates

A.S. Series — This was possibly the *Artistic Stationery Company* which provided both print and photographic cards over many years from the early 1900's.

BALMER /Kingston. — *S.J. Balmer, Stationers of 51 Kingston Hill, Kingston.* This retailer of their own-named cards traded from 1912 until 1928.

BABB — *Walter Richard. Confectioner, Stationer & Library at 133 Kingston Rd. New Malden* between pre-1921 and 1940.

CANNING'S Series. Stationers, 119 Malden Road. A series of about ten photographic cards published from 1936 by the original owner — *Miss Canning.* Today, the shop in the High Street retains the same name, but their old postcards are not so easy to find now. (Kingston Heritage Centre have copies of 2 or 3 from the named series.)

COLLECTORS' PUBLISHING CO. — *42/44 Imperial Buildings, Ludgate Circus, London E.C.* This was one of the largest distributors/agents for topographical postcards for S.W. London. It originally had offices in Fleet Street and the Company was active between 1901 and 1907. Their "MERCURY" series was the name printed on cards issued by the firm, to distinguish their *own* publications from others they handled.

HARTMANN — *Frederick.*, is most remembered for introducing the 'divided back' postcard around 1902. His Company published many types of cards between 1902-1909 from their London headquarters at *45 Farringdon St*

HIDE & Co. New Malden. Photographers &c. 17 Malden Road (On some earlier printed postcards *W.HIDE., Bookseller, 17 Market Place, New Malden.*) This was William Hide whose business, started in 1876, remained at this one address for over 60 years. Kelly's directories also show that he was the Verger at nearby Christ Church for 10 years from 1895. A picture of his shop circa 1935/6 appears on page 60. From pictures reproduced in the older copies of the *Surrey Comet* crediting *Hide & Co. New Malden*, it is now almost certain that the many handwritten captions on local cards reproduced here, and in the book "**Malden — Old & New**" (unless otherwise credited to *John's of Tooting, A.S. series, S. & W. series etc.*) identify *his* real photographic cards. Very few of these actually include his *name* as publisher, either on the fronts or backs of the cards. Being the local village photographers, *Hide & Co.* produced postcards of most of the major events, social occasions, and locations in the area. Without his prolific output, this book and others — and our local history generally, would be the poorer. [See also *MUNDAY, Henry .* below]

HUTCHINSON & Co. Wimbledon. Brief reference to this company found in Trim's local directory of Wimbledon for 1908/9. The address given for that year was *76a Hartfield Road.*

JOHNS-R.J. & Co., *171 Longley Rd., Tooting.* Another prolific photographic card publisher who covered much of the London area between 1911 and 1935, including New Malden.

J.T.B. Series — John T. Butterfield, Photographer, Cheam Road. Worcester Park [One reference found for 1907]

KINGSWAY REAL PHOTO. Series — this was a contemporary trade name for W.H.Smith's postcards.

KIRK — *Art Publisher, NewMalden.* Charles Joseph Kirk F.R.P.S. Photographic Art Publisher between 1898 and 1912. Mr Kirk, a Fellow of the Royal Photographic Society, produced a series of postcards of the area. His involvement with the local fire brigade started during the early days of his postcard publishing. His promotion to *Captain* by 1908, coupled with a gradual decline in demand for postcards at the end of the Edwardian era, possibly made him concentrate on his *Chief Officer of Fire Brigade* career, which continued until after 1936.

MUNDAY—Henry. Photographer. In 1907, lived in rooms above *HIDE'S* photographic shop. (*17 Malden Road*) From 1914 until at least 1940, he is given in Street Directories as *Harry Munday L.C.V. Professor of Music* at the same address. [He also gave violin lessons]. I have it on good authority that *Harry Munday* married *Hide's* daughter and carried on the photographic business after his death, but the dates of those events have yet to be researched.

PAYNE — *J.* -Stationer and Newsagent, 3 Market Place, (later No.6 Malden Rd.) New Malden from 1911 to 1923.

S. & W. Series — publisher not yet identified.

THOMAS — *Thomas. The Library,* (sic) *New Malden. Bookseller & Stationer at 4, Coombe Parade* (which later became No.19 Coombe Rd.) between 1905 and 1917. The monochrome series bearing his name was actually published by *HARTMANN*, [see above] and examples carry that trade mark.

Old Malden. — The Rectory *(Publ: Collectors' Publ. Co. Colour litho print. Postally used 1912)*

This Queen Anne vicarage was pulled down between 1934/5 and a new one less than half the size
built in its place.

OLD MALDEN

Old Malden Lane, Worcester Park.   *(Publ: S. & W. Series. No.179 Real Photo. Postally unused. c.1920's)*

This part of Old Malden Lane is known locally as Barrow Hill, after the name of the road leading off to the right. The brick pillar seen at the extreme left corner of the card marked the entrance to Barker's stables, and the nearby large house. When Edward VIII as Prince of Wales came to play polo at Motspur Park, he used a pony from these stables.

Old Malden Lane, Worcester Park. *(Publ: S. & W. Series No 247 Real Photo. Postally unused c.1920's)*

This card is the reverse view of that on the page opposite. The turning up to Barrow Hill is now on the left by the telegraph pole. I'm told that when these cottages were inhabited, the surnames of the occupants were [*from right to left*]: Bishop and Lister, and in another cottage set behind those shown here, the name of Symes. One Lucy Stokes lived in a house further on down the lane, and in the far distance off to the left, traces of Worcester Park House remain. In the days when all this land was part of the Nonsuch Palace estate, the Earl of Worcester was appointed Keeper of the 900 acre 'Great Park' — hence today's name *Worcester Park*.

Below: Today's view—the cottages on the right have been replaced by later buildings set further back from the road.

A Bit of Old Malden   *(Publ: Anon. B/W litho print. Postally used 1905)*

The 'bit' of Old Malden shown is *School Cottages* in what is now Church Road. Further along to the right, almost hidden behind the trees, is Malden Parochial School (1881). The man with the horse and cart doing the milk delivery round is believed to be from nearby New House Farm. In those days, a large churn on the back of the cart dispensed fresh milk straight into the cottagers' own jugs. A former occupier of the left hand cottage used to be Thomas Lock, the parish clerk. Part of his duty was the upkeep of St. John's churchyard. The Ordnance Survey map of 1868-70 shows *National School* and cottages marked. From that date, and right up until the 1920's, *Shiphouse Lane* emerged into Old Malden Lane (now Church Road) at this point — right opposite School Cottages. The 1898 edition of the map shows the name had become *Sheephouse Lane* remembered today in nearby *Sheephouse Way*. **Below**: Bing, the local Unigate milkman kindly recreated and completed the modern 'postcard' scene.

The Splash, Worcester Park. *(Publ: Anon. Real Photo. Postally unused. c.1910)*

The Splash was the open stretch of water between the railings beside the road, where horse and cart could just drive through for a short rest and watering before continuing a journey. Situated in Church Road, and known today as Plough Pond just in front of the famous old 'Plough Inn', this must have been a welcome and convenient 'watering hole' for horse and driver! Behind the coach and four is a shop selling refreshment of a different kind — R.Whites ginger beer, advertised on the enamel sign outside. (This is now the Italian restaurant in today's picture below.) The shop was run by a man affectionately known by local children as Mr 'Tubby' Hide. Next to the shop, on the right lived a Mr Taylor, who was by trade a builder and undertaker.

Old Malden. —
Footpath to Old Malden Church.
(Publ: Collectors' Publ. Co. Colour litho print. Postally used 1906)

The footpath was one of several leading to St. John's Church from different directions. Beyond the gate and bicycle, are the twin red roofs of the Vicarage [*or Rectory as the card on page 7 suggests*]. The church tower is hidden behind trees to the rear of the cottage at the left side of the footpath. The picture was taken from the corner where the top of Barrow Hill [*see page 8*] meets *The Royal Avenue* as it is shown on an early O.S. map.

Right: The same footpath is still there today, but the field shown above is now much overgrown to the left. To the right, running parallel to the path, a fence borders the back of a new housing development.

Devonshire Dairy Milk Delivery Cart*(Publ: probably Hide & Co. N.M. Real Photo. Postally unused. c.1908)*

Neither the location of the photograph, nor the identity of the fresh-faced young man has been discovered. Even his straw boater hatband advertises the business. The tin containers were used to carry a measure of milk from the churn on the cart to the customer's door. When it rained, it was not unusual for the lids to be removed so that the containers caught some rainwater. The milk was then added to the water collected in each measure, making it go a bit further on the round!

NEW MALDEN AT WORK

Montague Shopfront   *(Publ: Anon. Real Photo. Postally unused. Circa 1905)*

This highly detailed card shows the attractive window display of the baker and grocer's shop of Thomas Montague in *Market Place*. whose business can be traced back in the street directories to at least 1880.   When *Market Place* was absorbed into the road numbering system in 1912, his premises became No. 33 Malden Road, and the shop survived in his name until 1929.   By 1930, Ellis & Co. (Grocers) of Richmond had acquired the shop and traded there.   A large gaslight illuminates the entrance, while the window displays are highlighted by their own, smaller set of lamps inside the shop.   Among the groceries on show are 'Force' Wheat Flakes, Quaker Oats, and the large tins contain Ox Tongue or Fresh Lobster.   The shop also sold wines and spirits, notably Gilbey's gin. The first local volunteer fire service started over 100 years ago with Mr Montague in charge, his premises housing the simplest equipment.
Below: The shop premises still exist today — but as the *New Malden Rendezvous Restaurant* in the High Street.

Devonshire Dairy Milk Cart   *(Publ: Anon. Real Photo. Postally unused. Circa 1907-10)*

The Devonshire Dairy is first listed in street directories at *Market Place* in 1905, proprietor—Harry Sear. The dairy under Coleman & Son is listed from 1907 onwards.   The shop was between Hide's photographic shop [*see page 60*] and Fisher's hardware shop at the corner of Grafton Road. (Apex Tower offices now occupy the site).   From 1912 the address was 19 Malden Road; but by 1914, the firm had moved to other premises just up the road at No 39 [*see top of page 44*]. Again, the identity of the milkman is not known, but the plate below the cart-handle indicates this was *No.1* round. From 1922 the firm had an additional name incorporated— and was known as Coleman & Cole. They continued trading up to 1939 when they were presumably bought out — as in that year, H.A.Job Ltd. took over the dairy business at this address. Reproduced below is the design that was printed on the old, wide-mouth milk bottles of the later firm.

Unspecified Event   Market Place   *(Publ: Hide & Co. N.M. Real Photo. Postally unused. circa 1907-11)*

My guess is that this card records an Empire Day procession through Market Place. There are many children lining up, some with flags. Adults line the roadside and watch from the flat roofs above the shops. The date is between 1907, when the parade of shops beyond the fire station first opened (a hoarding near the roof advertises "SHOPS TO LET') and 1911, by which year a lamp-post had appeared on the corner of Grafton Road [*see page 54*]. The *Wood & Hill* shop on that corner, traded from these premises between 1890 and 1935. As a Grocers & Provision Merchants, they would have stocked bacon, hams and other fresh meats, cheese, eggs, dried fruits (currants, sultanas etc.) as well as the covenience foods in packets and tins. To the right of the door is a sticker advertising *Pure Butter 1/0* (i.e. 1 shilling, or 5 new pence) and that for a pound weight? Daily deliveries were made by horse and cart. [*see next page*]. The shop also stocked wines and spirits — as advertised regularly in the columns of the *Surrey Comet.*

Thetford Road New Malden   *(Publ: probably Hide & Co. N.M. Real Photo. Postally used 1908)*

This view of Thetford Road at its junction with Westbury Road includes the horse and cart of Wood & Hill, (the name is painted on the side above the wheel). A young lad accompanies the driver, possibly on the delivery round.

New Malden, Poplar Grove   *(Publ: Collectors' "Mercury" Series. Colour litho print. Postally used 1909)*

This card of Poplar Grove features one of the older Victorian residences — Cambridge House, partly hidden behind the high hedge to the left. The house itself faces the junction with Acacia Grove. John Hillard was listed in the 1908 and 1909 street directories at this address. In 1910 his occupation as a builder was first given, and he occupied the house with Miss Martha A. Hillard, *Dress Maker*. By 1921, there were still two occupants — Mrs Hillard with Miss Hillard, *Dress Maker*, and the house had been given the number 16. However, four years later, re-numbering caused it to become No.22, as it still is today, and the same occupants remained at the address until 1934/5.

[An elderly resident informed me that on Boxing Day, from around 1913 onwards, *The Groves* featured running races for adults as a general entertainment for the local people — a fit and healthy pastime after Christmas dinner?]

Below: Today's view. Cambridge House is behind the telegraph pole; the chimney stack has been partly removed.

ADVERTISEMENTS.

A WEST-END DRESSMAKER IN MALDEN.

Ladies, if you want all that is best in Dressmaking,
you **MUST** see

MISS HILLARD,

(Ten years' experience with leading West-end Firms)

Day and Evening Gowns.   Tailor-made Costumes.

Latest Styles and Fit Guaranteed.

Charges Strictly Moderate.

LADIES' OWN MATERIALS MADE UP.

ADDRESS:

CAMBRIDGE HOUSE, POPLAR GROVE

(FACING ACACIA GROVE).

Both advertisements reproduced here are from *Kelly's* Kingston and District street directory for 1910.

Originally, they each appeared on separate advertisement pages.

[*See also opposite page*]

30 years' **PRACTICAL** experience at your service.

J. HILLARD,

Builder, Contractor and House Decorator,

Poplar Grove, NEW MALDEN.

Alterations and Repairs of every description.

PAINTING AND DISTEMPERING.

Plumbing, Gas and Hot Water Fitting.

SANITARY WORK IN ALL BRANCHES.

ESTIMATES FREE.

No. 1029.   NEW MALDEN:—COOMBE ROAD

New Malden: — Coombe Road   *(Publ: Hutchinson & Co. Wimbledon. Real Photo. No.1029. Postally used 1907)*

What we now know as the *High Street* used to be called Malden Road, and prior to 1904 — Coombe Road. An even earlier map of 1866 shows Traps Lane as then extending beyond the railway bridge into Market Place. This scene of about 1907 was taken after the tram service extended to Raynes Park. The houses on the left were known as *Derby Villas* (not listed after 1911). *No.6 Derby Villas* was named 'The Laboratory' — the home of James Alfred Wanklyn MRCS, a famous professor of chemistry who died there in July 1906. One of the most noted organic chemists in the country, he also gained great respect and recognition abroad. In 1869 came his proudest honour, the Diploma of the Bavarian Academy — he and Faraday were 2 of only 4 such holders of an award rarely bestowed upon a foreigner. His food analyses methods were adopted here, in India, South Africa and the U.S.A. His *Ammonia Process* enabled chemists the world over, to earn vast sums — yet ironically, he died a comparatively poor man.

Malden Road, New Malden.   *(Publ: Anon. Colour litho print. Postally used — stamps unfranked. c.1930's)*

A later view from further down Malden Road than that shown opposite. The man in the foreground right is crossing Blagdon Road. In the middle distance on the left is the domed turret of The Plaza cinema, making the date pre-1936. Prior to 1908, when Sussex Road was named and had houses built, the only road entering Malden Road between Cambridge Road and the main Kingston Road was *Gloster Road*. It came into Malden Road opposite Blagdon Road. This appears to have lasted for pedestrian access at least, until 1922, as street directories for 1923 no longer give reference to Gloster Road (*i.e. off Malden Road*). Today, a small part of that original road remains between Connaught Road and Cleveland Road.

Below: Road widening in progress during Spring 1991 to improve traffic flow at the junction with Blagdon Road.

Malden Road New Malden   *(Publ: Cannings Series No.4. Real Photo. Postally unused. c.1936)*

This view must be from about 1936, when Miss Canning's shop first opened at No.119 Malden Road, and a series of their own-name postcards went on sale.   The Plaza cinema — which burned down at the end of 1936 — is seen on the left, and is today the site of McDonald's restaurant. The United Dairies shop on the right (now the A.A. local office) was also a local depot for milk distribution. The chemist's shop next to it — then owned by Davis & Davis, is now owned by J.T. Herman.

Malden Road New Malden   *(Publ: Hide & Co. N.M. Real Photo. Postally used 1912)*

This view is the reverse of the one shown opposite, but much earlier—around 1912. The parade of shops on the left is between the fire station and King's Avenue. The buildings were completed and opened as numbers *29 to 43 Malden Road* in 1907, when four shops were initially occupied. They were **No29**: Farebrother & Son, *Funeral Directors*; **No35**: Geddes, *Dyer and Cleaner*; **No39**: A.Anson & Co., *Ladies Outfitters*; and **No43**: Walter Coombes & Son, *Confectioner*. The 1912 re-numbering of Malden Road made all the shops in the parade even- numbered and were as above [*left to right*] **No40**: Madame Louise, *Milliner*; **No42**: W.N.Brooker, *Watchmaker*; **No44**: Mrs Frewer, *Confectioner*; **No46**: Thomas Reynolds, *China and Glass*; **No48**: Clarendon Dairy; **No50**: Mme. Alphonsine Sage, *Costumier*; **No52**: *Not listed*; **No54**: Walter Coombes & Son, *Confectioners*; **No56**: Freeman, Hardy & Willis, *Boots and Shoes*; **No58**: Boot's Cash Chemist; **No60**: *Not listed*; **No62**: Mrs Ward, *Furniture Dealer*. (Latter now Nat.West. Bank)

The Station New Malden   *(Publ: probably Hide & Co. N.M. Real Photo.No.4084. Postally unused. Circa 1908-10)*

This was opened on 1st December 1846, seventeen years before Kingston had its own station; but it was not until 1869 that the branch line from New Malden to Kingston was opened. By the mid-1880's, a hundred trains a day were calling at the station, but they had not always been so frequent. The residents of Coombe definately hadn't welcomed the development of a new town right on their doorstep, and had sufficient influence initially, to persuade the railway company to allow only three trains a day to stop here. The 'timetable' had improved to seven by 1857, but by late Victorian times the first impression of the town for rail passengers, was reflected in the dirty and dangerous state of the station! Mr Alfred Chalkley was the stationmaster at the time of this postcard, and it may be he who is standing towards the right of the centre platform—whose buildings have long since disappeared.

Albert Road   New Malden *(Publ: probably Hide & Co. N.M. Real Photo. No.6004. Postally unused. Circa 1908-13)*
A map of 1913 indicates that this block of twelve houses was the first to be erected in Albert Road; grass is still covering much of the unmade road.   The same map shows a *proposed* 'Vincent Road' adjacent to Albert Road, running between it and alongside part of Beverley Brook, joining Burlington Road opposite Beverley Road. This road was probably never adopted, as a later map of the 1920's shows Rapsons Tyre Works on that same site, followed in the 1930's by the Decca Gramophone and Record Works building. Today, the same site is the location of the B & Q DIY store and car park — just out of picture right [*below*]. In the background, Burlington Road Schools were opened in April 1908, but the frontage of the original buildings has changed somewhat over recent years. Today, 3 of the 5 classroom rooves seen above remain, following fire damage some years ago. [*See also page 26*]

"Empire Day" New Malden 1912 *(Publ: probably Hide & Co. N.M. Real Photo. Postally unused)*

This is the Burlington Road School front playground with pupils and staff lined up around the flagpole — which presumably is the focus of attention on Empire Day. The top of the flagpole is out of picture, so perhaps the Union Flag has just been, or is about to be raised. To the left in the background can be seen St. James' Mission Church, Burlington Road built in 1904, (now the site of the DSS building). Between this and the school building, is the open area of land occupied by Norbiton Pottery Works. The vertical poles behind the playground boundary are scaffolding poles about to be put to use as another building is squeezed in along Burlington Road.

Below: Today, the front area of the school is used as a staff car park, and interestingly, the camera was able to record the same number of classroom rooves as above — the only three that remain after a fire which seriously damaged the original buildings, one part of which [*shown opposite*] was completely replaced with new accommodation.

Surrey Comet May 1912

EMPIRE DAY

Celebrations at the Schools in the District

Patriotic Children

'Yesterday must have been a glad day for the Earl of Meath, to whom we are indebted for the proposal to adopt the birthday of our great Queen Victoria as Empire Day, for the idea "caught on" from the very first, and year by year has increased its hold upon the imagination of the English-speaking race, until now in every part of our mighty empire May 24th evokes a manifestation of loyalty and patriotism which must do much to link the various units of the empire indissolubly together.

In Kingston there was, as usual, a brave display of the national colours. The Union Jack floated proudly from church towers and public buildings, as well as from many private windows and flagstaffs. But one of the most important objects aimed at in the celebration of Empire Day is to impress upon the rising generation their duty to King and country, and in few places is this work more systematically undertaken than in this borough. As in previous years the Mayor and other members of the Education Committee devoted most of the day to visiting the elementary schools, in each of which there was a special celebration suited to the occasion, some account of which will be found below. Nor were the secondary schools at all lacking in their enthusiasm for Empire Day.......'

[At this point, there are individual reports of how many of the junior schools in the Kingston area spent their time celebrating Empire Day. Unfortunately, Burlington Road School was overlooked that year for some reason, so we can only guess how it was celebrated there, from the activity in the playground scene on the page opposite]

"Empire Day" New Malden 1912　　　　*(Publ: probably Hide & Co. N.M. Real Photo. Postally unused)*

Shannon Corner. New Malden. *(Publ: Anon. Real Photo. No. N.M.11. Postally used 1939)*

The Kingston by-pass, officially opened near this spot by Stanley Baldwin in 1927, at its junction with Burlington Road shows crossroads controlled by traffic lights. Even before the many, more recent improvements were made, the then Prime Minister hoped there would be adequate facilities to cope with the casualties of what had already been described nationally as Britain's "Suicide Road".   The name — *Shannon Corner* — came from the Shannon Office Equipment building, [*out of picture left, where today the Queensway furniture warehouse stands*] which was in operation between the 1930's and 1970's. Across the by-pass is the Duke of Cambridge public house —today almost hidden by the elevated section of the A3.   On the corner where this picture was taken used to be the huge Odeon cinema. The trolley bus wires overhead show the route along the continuation of Burlington Road to Raynes Park.

MOTOR ACCIDENT JULY 30/14   NEW MALDEN

Motor Accident July 30th 1914 New Malden   *(Publ: Hide & Co. N.M. Real Photo. Postally unused)*

This accident happened in Malden Road at the entrance to Malden College (which was opposite the end of Thetford Road). The policemen and two men behind the car are the only ones smiling for the camera! Unfortunately, no report was found in the *Surrey Comet* for the week following this event. However, the following headline was observed in that same week's edition:

Motor Traffic on Surrey Roads

'Heavy motors have quadrupled and ordinary cars and motor cycles doubled in five years on Surrey roads, beside which there has been an enormous incursion of motor omnibuses.'

ACCIDENT AND EMERGENCY

House Fire — Blagdon Road.   *(Publ: Anon. probably Hide & Co. N.M. Real Photo. Postally used 1906.)*

The crowd watching the fire brigade attempting to put out the fire, is standing on the open land between Burlington and Blagdon Roads.   At this time, and until 1930's it was a sports/cricket field with its own pavilion.   Malden Wanderers Cricket Club had their home here from their inception in 1879.   Later, when the land was developed, the club moved to premises in Cambridge Avenue, where they now field hockey, tennis and badminton teams as well as cricket. [*see also p.62*]   Today of course, that land is occupied by the Blagdon Road car park, shops and offices, the Malden Centre complex, Fountain T.V. studios and the postal sorting office.

Bad news has always travelled fast, it seems — not just by word of mouth or in newspapers. To accompany the report of The Fire in the *SURREY COMET for Saturday July 21st 1906,* advertisers had not been slow to buy the immediately following column space to try to sell their fire insurance.

VILLA BURNED OUT

Firemen handicapped by Shortage of Water Supply.

One of the most serious fires seen in Malden for many years broke out on Saturday morning at 1, Blagdon Road. The house, a substantially built villa owned by Mr V. Davison, is situated at the corner of Howard and Blagdon roads, and was in the occupation of Mrs Ellen Esser, who, at about twenty minutes to twelve in the morning, was engaged in trimming lamps. By some means the oil drum, filled with paraffin, became upset and exploded. Immediately the room was in flames, and Mrs Esser, who was the only person in the house at the time, rushed out.

The alarm was given at the fire station by the next-door neighbour. Within a few minutes, the brigade, consisting of Deputy-Captain Kirk (officer in charge) and fourteen men, arrived on the scene, and promptly got to work. The house was then fully ablaze, and efforts were made to prevent the fire from spreading to the adjoining property. In this the brigade were successful, as although practically the whole of the furniture and effects were destroyed at No.1, Blagdon road, little damage except by water was sustained at the next house, Laburnham-villa, owned and occupied by Mr C.W. Keeping.

At the outset the brigade were handicapped in consequence of the supply of water from the hydrant being quite insufficient to cope with the flames, which had taken a strong hold of the house. Some little time elapsed before the arrival of the turncock, and then a full supply of water was obtained from the main road. By one o'clock, however, the fire was practically extinguished, but not before the house had been gutted. Meanwhile a band of helpers had been engaged in removing the furniture from the next house, and the roadway was soon packed with furniture of every description, much of it being considerably damaged through having been thrown out of the upper windows. The Kingston and Surbiton Fire Brigades, in charge of Superintendants Drury and Hards, who had been summoned privately by telephone, arrived on the scene with their steamers, but their services were not required, the local brigade having the fire under control when they arrived. The value of the house and furniture is happily covered by insurance. Throughout Saturday and Sunday a large number of people visited the scene of the outbreak.

———————————————

FIRE ! FIRE !! FIRE !!! - Why lose your property? Insure against loss or damage by fire. Annual premium 1s 6d. per £100 for property, and 2s. per £100 for furniture - Messrs E. Hudson & Co., Auctioneers, Surveyors, House and Estate Agents, Station Yard, New Malden, undertake insurances of every description. Call or write for full particulars and prospectus. Houses to be let or sold. Auctions arranged. - [ADVT.]

———————————————

INSURE against Fire in the SUN FIRE OFFICE - Full particulars of W.G. Sudbury & Sons, Agents, 5 & 7, Market place, New Malden. - [ADVT.]

"After the Storm. Oct 2nd 1913"   *(Publ. Probably Hide & Co. New Malden. Real Photo. Postally used 1913)*
Grafton Road had originally been named *Providence Place* — it is said, because providence was always necessary when crossing it!   Senior citizens can still remember the days when it used to flood regularly in wet weather or after a cloudburst.   A full account of the effects of this storm on the borough appears opposite.   In the view above, the shops on the right disappeared when Apex Tower and its car park were erected in the mid-1960's.   In 1913, the shops consisted of **No4**: George Hay, *Fishmonger*; **No6**: Isaac Burton, *Provision Dealer*; **No8**: Walter S. Booker, *Greengrocer*; **No10**: William C. Rimington, *Confectioner*; **No12**: Magnus Deinhardt, *Hairdresser*.   The houses on the extreme left leading up to Avenue Road, had all been replaced by the 1980's with a new housing development laying back to Tregarron Gardens.   The picture below was taken on the day following the fire of 18th March 1991 when the High Street was closed, parking restricted and all traffic including buses, diverted down Grafton Road.

Surrey Comet - Sat. October 4th 1913 page 7

HEAVY THUNDERSTORM
Extraordinary Scenes in the District

TRAMS AND BUSES HELD UP
Children's Difficulties in Getting to School

HOUSES STRUCK BY LIGHTNING

The summer-like weather which marked the last week in September was broken in Kingston in a sensational manner on Thursday, the storm being of a severity quite without parallel in the recent history of the borough.

Shortly after noon the sky became overcast from a northerly direction, but it was not until a few minutes before 1 o'clock that rain fell, increasing in violence with such rapidity that immediate shelter became necessary.

The downpour was of such intensity that within the period of 1 hour nearly an inch and a half of rain was registered, or much more than sometimes falls in a whole month.

Almost as soon as the rain began a terrific flash of lightning was the precursor of a thunderstorm which continued with unabated violence for nearly three quarters of an hour, the lightning being remarkably vivid and the peals of thunder almost deafening.

Such an immense volume of water pouring on to the streets had the natural effect of temporarily choking the drains. Thoroughfares that have hitherto borne an irreproachable character for non-flooding became almost impassable and where roadways dipped to allow more headroom for bridges the water varied from a foot to nearly six times this depth.

In practically every part of the borough the story was the same, people being unable to enter or leave their houses unless they walked through water. Many business premises had flooded basements, in some cases there being serious damage to stock.

There were places along the tram routes where the cars divided the water something akin to the progress of a fast moving steamer.

Various houses in the area were struck with varying degrees of damage including a New Malden residence which escaped lightly.

Of those children caught at home out of school for dinner, the few who arrived back at school to find playgrounds like lakes, were so bedraggled that they were sent home early by staff.

Damage at New Malden

There was a sensational rainfall at New Malden, 1.20 inches being registered in 24 minutes. the deluge which lasted for about half an hour, seriously damaged some of the roads in the village. The Kingston road, near the railway bridge, was flooded to a depth of nearly 5 feet, and in Cambridge road there was a fast flowing stream into Malden road which washed a considerable amount of mud into the drains and choked them.

The action of the water also demolished a portion of the fence which encloses the Wesleyan Church. Council workmen were soon engaged in remedial measures, and the water gradually diminished, but all pedestrian and a great deal of vehicular traffic was held up for some time. On the Kingston road the passage of tramcars was made extremely difficult, and after the water had subsided a great deal of mud was left on the road and footpath.

Footnote:
During the preparation of this book, in the early hours of Monday 18th March 1991, New Malden suffered its worst ever fire —causing millions of pounds worth of damage to the new shopping precinct centred around and incorporating the facade of the old Town Hall. Ironically, the fire is thought to have started in premises, the site of which was the location of the town's first fire station. Eighty firefighters, some from as far away as Hillingdon, Heston, Clapham, Chelsea and Croydon attended the scene. Some of the pictures on following pages were taken during the course of that Monday.

Tram Accident   Kingston Rd.   New Malden   June 8th 1911 *(Publ: Hide & Co. N.M. Real Photo. Postally unused)*
"A collision which might have been fraught with serious consequences occurred on Thursday evening near Cambridge Terrace, Kingston Road, New Malden.   A tramcar was proceeding towards Kingston, when a heavy motor lorry, owned by Messrs Friary, Holroyd and Healey, came out from a side-turning and collided with the front of the car.   As a result the front platform of the tram mounted the near front wheel of the lorry, locking the two vehicles together. The car body was canted over, and some alarm was occasioned among the passengers who thought it would be overturned.   The weight of the trucks and undergear, however, proved quite sufficient to prevent such a catastrophe.   Kingston and Fulwell breakdown gangs were quickly on the spot, and by jacking up the front of the car, the lorry was extricated, both tracks being blocked for some time.   It was found that the vehicles had sustained little serious damage, and there were no personal injuries."*(Surrey Comet. Sat. June 10th 1911 p.7)*

New Malden Fire Brigade   *(Publ: Hide & Co. New Malden. Real Photo. Postally unused. Circa 1914)*
Posing proudly on their first motorised fire-engine outside the fire station and Town Hall, are the fire crew. On the sides of the vehicle the words: 'Malden & Coombe Urban District Council'. It appears that the brigade acquired their new 'First Aid' motor [*see report next page*] in 1914, some time after Kingston made their decision to buy two such engines in 1909. Then, Kingston had invited tenders from suppliers: most expensive was Messrs Shand, Mason & Co. at £1,295 each; the accepted / lowest price was from Messrs Dennis Bros. at £870 each. Messrs Merryweather & Sons Ltd. (He of New Malden) had weighed in at £1,045 and £920! The horse-drawn 'steamer' continued in use in New Malden after 1914, but due to the war effort the *Surrey Comet* of Sept. 12th 1914 reported *'the military authorities taking from the Surveyor's Department, the two horses used for horsing the fire engine, for which they paid £35 each.'* The recommendation by the council was that *'a suitable replacement horse should be purchased for the sum of £45.'*

New Malden Fire Brigade   *(Publ: Hide & Co. New Malden. Real Photo. Postally unused. Circa 1914)*

FIRE AT MOTSPUR PARK — Smart work by the Malden Fire Brigade. *(Surrey Comet — Sept. 12th 1914 p.8)*
'What threatened to be a disastrous fire was, by the prompt action of the New Malden Fire Brigade, last Saturday evening completely got under in less than two hours. At the time of the outbreak the Fire Brigade was participating in the mass meeting at Beverley Park to obtain recruits for Lord Kitchener's New Army, when a call was given by maroon to a fire at the residence of Captain Malcolm, Old Farm House, Motspur Park, who is away on active service. With a full crew of 18 men, under the command of Captain Kirk [*next to driver*] the motor engine proceeded to the scene of the conflagration which is a large old-fashioned residence with a new addition, and containing 26 rooms. The Brigade arrived within 3 minutes of the call. A great factor in this good "stop" was undoubtedly the First-Aid motor, proving again its usefulness as a fire-fighting machine.' **Below:** A modern emergency call-out.

Council Buildings. New Malden. *(Publ: Anon. No.NM.8. Real Photo. Postally used in 1941)*
Showing part of the original fire station next to the Town Hall — comparison of the access doors in both these facing-page cards illustrates that the entrances to the fire station had to be enlarged to accomodate the engines as they increased in size. The 1914 fire-engine shown opposite, has been photographed outside the middle of 3 doors each of which clearly has an 'arched' top, beneath a sloping, tiled roof. In the card above, the doors have been heightened and squared off at the top. To make this possible, the front of the sloping roof has been removed and a brick facade built above the doors. The reason for drawing attention to this is another consideration that the fire brigade would have had to make — the railway arch. Even in the 'steamer' days, firemen on board had to 'duck' their heads to negotiate this hazard! As early as 1913, the *Surrey Comet* reported a meeting when councillors referred to 'the black hole of Malden', and its need for improvement. The arch was enlarged between 1959-61.

Police Station New Malden   *(Publ: probably Hide & Co. N.M. No.4001.Real Photo. Postally unused. c.1908-10)*
Looking rather isolated in this picture taken after 1907, the Police Station was opened in 1891 — so this year is celebrating its centenary. Before New Malden had a police station, local offenders had had to be accompanied on foot to Wimbledon, Kingston or Epsom stations! Externally, the building appears to have changed very little in its lifetime; inevitably, more shops and houses now adjoin its location at the corner of Burlington Road and High Street. Today, the number of police officers attached to the station is significantly less than that recorded in the picture opposite — which was taken in the yard behind the building. Currently there are five home-beat officers based at New Malden.

"V Division Malden Section 1910"   *(Publ: Hide & Co. N.M. Real Photo. Postally unused. c.1910)*

Of the 35 policemen in the photograph, only one is without a moustache! There appear to be eight sergeants, one of whom is probably the station sergeant — 'O. Fisher'. Also in the front row, one plain-clothes officer is wearing plus fours. The constable on the extreme left is believed to be P.C. Whipp who patrolled along South Lane — one side of which came under New Malden police, and the other side of the road under Surbiton police. It was an offence to park a car at night without lights, and those residents of South Lane with such cars would exploit the police boundary by first parking on the side patrolled by P.C. Whipp when the *Surbiton* P.C. was doing his evening patrol, and then run out to re-park their cars on the Surbiton side before P.C. Whipp arrived on *his* last patrol, thus avoiding being "booked" for illegal parking!

Below: The police and fire service were kept busy when the High Street was closed for several days after *the fire*.

The Fountain New Malden Damaged April 28th 1914　　　*(Publ: Hide & Co. Real Photo. Postally unused)*
'Malden Fountain Damaged'　　*Surrey Comet Saturday May 2nd 1914*　　[*Today's photo taken February 1991*]
'The fountain at New Malden, which was erected some years ago by the Band of Mercy, was seriously damaged on Tuesday. The horses attached to a pair-horse van laden with timber were drinking at the trough, and in turning away the animals caused a piece of the heavy timber to strike the column of the fountain. A boy who was in the vicinity had a narrow escape. He was drinking at the fountain and, seeing the impending danger ran, but tripped over kerbing, grazing his knee.' (The fountain used to have a copper mug on a chain for human refreshment, but competing nearby at around this time used to be a hot drinks stall selling cocoa at a halfpenny a cup!)
The quotation on the base of the fountain reads: 'A righteous man regardeth the life of his beasts' Proverbs XII.I0
Below: The roundabout protects today's ornamental fountain against most things—except of course, the weather!

(Publ: Hide & Co. N.M. Real Photo. Postally used 1915)

New Malden A.V.F. March to Oxshott. March 21st 1915

WAR &
PEACE

New Malden A.V.F.   March to Oxshott   Mch. 21st 1915   *(Publ: Hide & Co. N.M. Real Photo. Postally used 1915*

VOLUNTEERS ON THE MARCH

'The Malden Companies of the First Fifth Battalion of the Surrey Volunteers had a day's route march on Sunday and acquitted themselves well, covering over 20 miles, and carrying rifles and laden haversacks.   The principal halt was made at Oxshott, where, after outposts had been placed, the cooks served up an appetising meal of stew. The march was a great success and proved thoroughly enjoyable.'   *Surrey Comet, Sat. March 27th 1915*

Group of Sergeants New Malden A.V.F. April 25th 1915 *(Publ: Hide & Co. N.M. Real Photo. Postally unused)*
Although referred to by the publisher on his cards as the 'A.V.F.', the *Surrey Comet* of *May 1st 1915* records the Officers of A and B Companies of this, the 1st Battalion 5th Surrey *Volunteer Training Corps*. Accompanying the photograph is a report as follows: 'From to-day the A and B Companies of the 1st /5th Battalion (Wimbledon) Surrey V.T.C. will be in possession of a rifle range of their own, but to-day's ceremonial on the ground in Cambridge Avenue by no means completes the work of the Companies, and no member will be satisfied until the range at 100 yards is fully equipped. General Sir Josceline Wodehouse G.C.B., C.M.G., R.A., Commandant of the Surrey Regiment, will perform the opening ceremony, at which it is expected a large company will be present. The band from the East Surrey Regimental Depot, Kingston Barracks, will be in attendance.'
Section Commanders New Malden A.V.F. April 25th 1915 *(Publ: Hide & Co. N.M. Real Photo. Postally unused)*

Recruiting at New Malden October 2nd 1915   *(Publ: Hide & Co. New Malden. Real Photo. Postally unused)*

Just out of picture left is the old Wesleyan Chapel on the corner of Cambridge Road. The shopfronts in Malden Road (now High Street) from left to right are: **No 41**: Chas. W. Price, *Boot manufacturer and repairer* /George Willett, *Confectioner/Tobacconist*; **No 39**: Walter Coleman & Sons, *Devonshire Dairy* located previously in Market Place [*page 13*] between Hide's photographic shop and Fisher's Oilman/Hardware shop [*see* 'Malden—Old & New' *page 47*]. These new Dairy premises opened at this location in 1914. **No 37**: Read & Co. *Motor Engineers*; **No 35**: Ernest A. Horwood, *Fishmonger and Poulterer*. Just out of picture right, was **No 33**: Thomas Montague's *Baker's* shop [*see page 14*] **Below**: The same shopfronts — but today's view. An Estate Agents replaces E.A. Horwood's shop. *Surrey Cameras* now stands in place of Read & Co., and the Devonshire Dairy frontage is now *FarmcRaft* Film Distributors. Other premises boarded over await new owners.

SURREY COMET Sat. October 9th 1915:

GREAT RECRUITING RALLY

Procession of Troops Through Surbiton and Kingston.

HIGH SHERIFF AT NEW MALDEN

A display of bunting in the vicinity of the Council Offices, and at the headquarters of the 5th Battalion of the Volunteer Training Corps, proclaimed the fact that Malden was on the alert last Saturday in connection with the great recruiting rally. Fortunately there was a suspension of rain during the actual proceedings in the afternoon, and quite a large crowd gathered in front of the Council Offices where, adjacent to the fire-station, a platform had been erected. Members of the Council with the Chairman, Mr. Harold Bailey J.P., had assembled to welcome the High Sheriff, Mr. C.Tyrrell Giles K.C., and they occupied seats on the dais. There was also present a strong detachment from the 5th Battalion of the Surrey V.T.C. under the command of Mr. H.G.Robertson, though the main body had proceeded to Wimbledon. Accompanying the Volunteers were a number of Red Cross nurses attached to the 5th Battalion, with them being Mrs. Porter, Miss Redford, Mrs Speirs and Mrs. Hurst.

Mr. Harold Bailey introduced the High Sheriff, who was heartily applauded on rising to speak on the urgent need of getting more men. At the close of what was quite a brief period of speech making, in which Mr.G.R.Johnson (V.T.C.) and others took part, a vote of thanks was accorded to the High Sheriff, followed by the singing of the National Anthem. Afterwards the High Sheriff inspected the volunteers on parade, to several of whom he spoke.

An Interesting Letter.

From Pte. High of the East Surrey Regiment, a letter has been received by Mr. J.W.Johnson, by whom the arrangements for Saturday's meeting were made. Pte. High writes:-

"I have only just received your letter re the recruiting rally to be held tomorrow. If it had been next Saturday I could have managed to get there. Quartered as I am in what they term the war area, one sees what our race is made of. Whilst out on guard here

in the long dark hours of the night, it is most weird to hear reveille sounded at 3 a.m., and about 40 minutes later a band starts up with "Who's your lady friend?" or "Thumbs up" amid cheers and shouts, all the while getting nearer and louder, and presently a draft of Fusiliers or Buffs or East Surreys come into a very dim view. We have no lights here, so although they, these noble lads, are passing within a few feet, they are not distinguishable (nor even extinguishable). They leave with hearts as light and gay as any Sunday school excursion. At 4 a.m. one hears in the distance "Auld Lang Syne," and another batch have gone to fight for a righteous cause. It really makes the most flint-hearted soften. It makes one sincerely proud to claim these young fellows as brother countrymen. The country can never be in any danger so long as this splendid spirit prevails. It is difficult to understand why recruiting rallies are necessary. Is it not the grandest thing possible to go forth and fight your country's battle?............"

The Maldens and Coombe Military Band (*Publ: Hide & Co. New Malden. Real Photo. Postally unused. Circa 1914*)

NEW MALDEN AND COOMBE
WORKMEN'S MILITARY BAND.

A FETE

Will be held on BANK HOLIDAY, AUGUST 3rd, in
THE GROUNDS OF COOMBE HOUSE,
Kindly lent by W.J. Compton, Esq.

Grand variety of amusements, Athletic Sports, &c.
Grounds open at 2. Admission by Programme, 6d. Children
half-price

Surrey Comet report of 8th August 1896
WORKMEN'S BAND FETE

'Under the auspices of the New Malden and Coombe Workmen's Military Band a very successful fete was held on Bank Holiday in the meadow adjoining Coombe House, which was kindly lent by Mr.W.J.Compton. At one o'clock a procession was formed at the drinking fountain, those taking part being members of the Court "Malden" A.O.F., a London lodge of the Ancient Order of Shepherds, and the members of the District Council Fire Brigade, with their manual. These headed by the band and followed by a large crowd of persons marched through the village to the grounds, which were thrown open at 2pm. The committee had made extensive arrangements for the enjoyment of the large company which assembled. Several tents, refreshment booths and a stand for the band were erected, the materials being lent by Mr J.Earle. Roundabouts, shooting galleries, cocoa nut shies &c., were all well patronised during the afternoon and evening, the attendants being kept well employed. Refreshments were supplied during the day by Mr Hampton and Mr Pryor; the band played

at intervals; and a couple of acrobats from London gave two performances of about ten minutes duration. The members of the fire brigade gave exhibition of their drill, under the direction of Capt. Davison, and these were watched with much interest by the spectators. In addition to this a short list of athletic sports was gone through, and caused considerable amusement. One event was a smoking contest, and caused some genuine fun. The competitors had to place their tobacco, pipe and matches on a form, which was 150 yards from the starting point. At a given signal they had to run to the form, fill their pipe and commence smoking. L. Petit accomplished this in the shortest time and became the winner of the first prize; besides the more conventional races for children, other events included a 50 yards race for men over 60; an obstacle race; and a stone picking race. The remaining contest was a tug of war between the band and the firemen. The conditions were ten a-side, first two out of three. The band were the heaviest team and pulled their opponents over the line twice in succession. During the day there was a cart horse parade, and prizes were awarded to Mr Tarvin and Mr Roberts for the best kept animals. Owing to rain one or two events had to be abandoned, but there was no lack of amusement at any time during the evening. Dancing formed one of the attractions, and the prizes were distributed in one of the tents by the Vicar, who addressed a few appropriate words to the competitors. A word of praise is due to the committee, Messrs. F.Earl, F.Harris, R.Hutchins, L.Crandley, E.Ansell and J.Plumbridge, and to Mr J.Andrews and Mr J.Buzwell, the honorary secretaries, for their untiring energy to make the affair the success that it was. After paying the expenses about £11 will be handed over to the band funds.'

March through Market Place New Malden. *(Publ: Hide & Co. N.M. Real Photo. Postally unused. c.1915)*

THE CAMP IN RICHMOND PARK *(Surrey Comet May 8th 1915)*
6000 London Territorials in Training.   Excellent Conditions.   The Skirl of the Bagpipes.

'........while our reporter was there he witnessed an inspiring spectacle in the return from a long route march of the London Scottish who were led by the regimental mascot—a large deerhound—and headed by the band of pipers. The men looked in the pink of condition, and as they swung into the camp appeared fit for the endurance of any hardships.' (Unfortunately, there is nothing to link this part of the report directly to the postcard itself, except to show that the London Scottish Regiment were in the area in May 1915.)

Below: 1959-61 saw road widening for enlargement of the railway bridge, and later, the tower office block nearby.

Peace Celebrations New Malden July 19th 1919 No.14   *(Publ: Hide & Co. N.M. Real Photo. Postally unused)*

Surrey Comet Sat. 26th July 1919

MALDEN'S FESTIVAL

A Happy Time for Over 3,000 Children.

Commemorative Medal

Children first, children last, was the theme of the Peace celebrations festivities at Malden on Saturday, which proceeded without a hitch until the rain in the early evening compelled a cessation of open-air proceedings.

The scholars and others had been requested to assemble outside the Council offices at 1.20 prior to marching in procession to the Beverley park, where the festivities were to be held. At 1.30. headed by the band of the Norbiton and Kingston Hill Cadet companies, the column moved off headed by the local Troop of Boy Scouts, the local fire brigade, Council officials, local clergy, members of local organisations and the general committee of the Peace celebrations. Then came the school children, Burlington road infants, Elm road and Lime grove infants; Dickerage lane infants and other schools were in the same order. A number of residents followed immediately behind the children, and the rear of the procession was brought up by the police and V.A.D. with motor ambulance. Crowds of residents assembled to witness the procession, which made a pretty picture, especially as it proceeded up the hill in Duke's avenue.

On arrival at the Park the children, about 3,000 in number, were formed in mass in front of a platform from which a short service was conducted by Canon W. A. Challacombe (Vicar) and other local clergy.

In a short address to the children, the Chairman of the Council said that day they were met to celebrate a peace which had come after the greatest war the world had ever known, and for that peace they were indebted to those who had responded to the call, and sacrificed everything in the cause of justice and freedom, and Malden had responded to that call as well as any district in the kingdom. (Applause) They (the children) would be the generation of the future, and as they became citizens of this glorious Empire it was for them to look back with pride upon those who had gained for them their heritage, and uphold it. So that that day might be more impressed on their memories, Mr Longworthy announced that Mr Typke had generously provided a victory and peace medal for each child. A representative from each department of the various schools then ascended the platform and amid loud applause Mr Typke pinned medals on their breasts.

The gathering, which meantime had increased to several thousands, broke away to take part in and watch the sports and other organised amusements. A comic football match, in which the players were attired in all kinds of costumes, caused much merriment, while Mr Cater, as a clown, was a great attraction throughout the afternoon, his comicalities creating no end of enjoyment.

At intervals during the afternoon the children were supplied with tea, the difficulties arising from the inability to secure a caterer being overcome by utilising the kitchens at Burlington road schools, where all the tea was brewed and conveyed in large urns to the grounds.

Following the sports, arrangements had been made by Mrs Hunter and Miss Rene Rayment to provide entertainments from 6.30 p.m., but unfortunately before that hour rain came on rather heavily. The Graham Spicer Institute was made available and for several hours packed audiences had the pleasure of listening to programmes of excellent merit. In the carrying out of the sports yeoman service was rendered by Mr Honey, headmaster of Burlington road schools, who was ably assisted by Mr Cole and others.'

(Then follows the results of the sports; separate races for boys and girls/infants and juniors)

The Decorations

In commemoration of the day the whole district was ablaze with decorations, for whichever way one turned flags, streamers and fairy lamps met the gaze. Specially artistic decorative skill marked the adornment of the front of the Council Buildings. On each side and about 10 feet from the ground were fixed large figures emblematical of victory, represented by angels holding aloft wreaths of laurel, from the centre of which electric lights shone, forming an imposing setting to hundreds of coloured fairy lamps, figures of Britannia, crowns and flags. All the emblematical designs were made locally at the Pytram Works. Streamers stretched from the top of the building to the fence, linking up with a generous display on the Graham Spicer Institute adjoining. The business premises of Mr Tudor Williams, at the junction of Malden road and Cambridge roads, was practically covered with fairy lamps, flags, streamers etc., making an effective show. [......continued over]

Peace Celebrations New Malden July 19th 1919 No.12 *(Publ: Hide & Co. N.M. Real Photo. Postally unused)*

Council Offices New Malden *(Publ: Hide & Co. N.M. Real Photo. Postally unused. c.1919)*

The Decorations *(cont. from p.49)* 'In spite of the rain, crowds of residents flocked into the Malden road in the evening to witness the illumination of the Council Buildings and the other premises mentioned, and as darkness came on that portion of the district at once became a blaze of light, which was augmented by the light from the shop windows, illuminated for the occasion. At intervals Capt. Kirk ignited coloured flares on the top of the fire tower at the fire station. Rough bands paraded along the street, and rockets, squibs, cannon crackers and other forms of fireworks flying about the road proved rather disconcerting to many onlookers. However, extraordinarily good feeling prevailed, everyone seemingly being out for enjoyment without horse-play. It was after midnight before the streets resumed their usual quietude.' **Below:** It was after midnight that a different blaze of light recently lit up the district, but there were no celebratory flares from the site of the old fire station — only investigations next day.

Welcome Home. New Malden Aug. 28th 1920 *(Publ: Hide & Co. N.M. Real Photo. Postally unused)*

Among the many distinguished guests, the postcard shows on the 'Welcome' platform - Standing: Major-General Sir J.R.Longley K.C.M.G. C.B. Seated to the left, Lady Longley (having been presented with a bouquet), and their daughter and son. Also seated at table right is Mr A. Woollacott J.P. (Chairman of the Council) and to the left behind him Mr J.W.Johnson M.B.E. (Clerk of the District Council and Honorary Secretary of the Organising Committee for the day's events). To the right, seated behind the standing scout are the Mayor and Mayoress of Wimbledon, Mr and Mrs Dudley Stuart.

"WELCOME HOME"   *Surrey Comet August 28th 1920*

To-day's Programme Outlined at Meeting of Ex-service Men

'Welcome Home' will be a civic function organised by representatives of the 18,000 inhabitants of the district. It is intended to be a feeling tribute to the unforgetable bravery of sailors, soldiers and airmen from New Malden, Old Malden and Coombe, who have endured hardships in the great and successful struggle for freedom. *(Then follows the order of proceedings)*

Subsequently the ex-servicemen will be entertained to tea, a sports programme will be carried out, musical entertainments including performances by the bands will be given, and an old English Fair and dancing will be other attractions. Through the generosity of the Wimbledon Borough Council the park will be illuminated by electric light.

Several of the local tradesmen have decided to close their premises from 1-5pm and it is hoped as many others as possible will follow this example.

Surrey Comet Sept. 4th 1920

'Apart from a little haziness of the sky better weather than that which favoured Saturday's rejoicings could not have been wished for. Many of the residents of Malden complied with the request of the Celebrations Committee and decorated their houses and business premises with flags and bunting so that the whole district presented an appearance befitting such an auspicious occasion.

The procession formed outside the council offices was headed by the Maldens and Coombe Fire Brigade on their first-aid motor appliance under the command of Captain Kirk and Second Officer Cullerne and the "Queen's Band" (Royal West Surrey Regiment, Guildford). These were followed by Major-General Longley and other distinguished visitors, members of the Urban District Council, Ex-Servicemen under Major White M.C., Special Constabulary Cadets, Malden Troop of Boy Scouts with Malden Military Band bringing up the rear. The route to the park was lined with spectators and a liberal display of flags and other decorations considerably added to the brilliance of the scene as the procession passed through the streets.'

Red Cross Hospital New Malden   *(Publ: Hide & Co. New Malden. Real Photo. Postally used 1916)*

This was the Springfield Branch hospital in Kingston Road which was refurbished and redecorated during 1915 for accommodating the returning wounded soldiers of the Great War.   All four wings of the building were used and postcard views of their interiors were made available for residents to communicate with distant relatives. Medical service was provided by local doctors, and concert parties for the patients were given occasionally by local people — one senior citizen can still remember once going there as a young girl, to dance at one of these events. More recently, the buildings were in use for elderly folk as the *Morris Markowe Unit*.   But the violent weather of recent years took its toll of the old buildings, particularly the rooves, and the hospital was completely demolished during February and March 1991, during which period the picture below was taken.

Malden's Charter
Celebrations 23.9.36

Malden's Charter Celebrations 23.9.36 No.2
(Publ: Anon.possibly Hide & Co. N.M. Real Photo. Postally unused)
The Lord Mayor of London and the Charter Mayor meet at the Beverley Bridge
borough boundary in Burlington Road before processing to the Town Hall.

CELEBRATION
& CEREMONY

Coronation Celebration New Malden June 23rd 1911 No.8   *(Publ: Hide & Co. Ltd. N.M. Real Photo. Unused)*

Surrey Comet Saturday June 24th 1911

YESTERDAY'S CELEBRATIONS

Memorial Clock Unveiled

'New Malden was all agog with excitement and animation on Friday, for the inhabitants were evidently determined not to be behind in a display of loyalty, and the village presented quite an animated and festive appearance. The critics who declare Malden to be a sleepy little place, lacking in enterprise have been forever confounded. The decorations excelled those in many other districts, there being a splendid spirit of co-operation displayed, and there were few houses that had not some attempt, however small, at decoration and illumination. The Norbiton Arms (*sic*) Hotel presented a gay appearance with flags and bunting and the houses down to the railway bridge were nearly all decorated, but it was the Council Offices that attracted most attention, for they were a real picture. Four large posts, decorated with bunting, and a shield bearing the letters "G.R." had been placed in the garden in front of the offices and from them depended streamers of flags,

artistically arranged. The offices were also tastefully adorned with flags and fairy lamps. At the front of the tower was a green flag bearing the words 'A Tribute to Loyalty' covering the clock which was shortly to be unveiled.

The band of the 3rd Battalion East Surrey Regiment under Mr W. Schafer, struck up a martial air, and at its conclusion Mr A.T.E. Mursell (Chairman, Maldens & Coombe District Council) advanced to the door of the Council Offices, preparatory to unveiling the clock.

Mr Mursell said the first function to be performed in common with their celebration of the Coronation was the unveiling of a public clock that had been presented to New Malden by one of its residents. That gentleman was very modest, and did not wish his name disclosed. They had long needed a public clock for New Malden and they greatly appreciated the kindness and generosity of this anonymous donor. Mr Mursell then pulled the cord which released the covering flag, amidst loud cheers, revealing to view a very handsome clock. The clock was provided by Mr W.N. Brooker of New Malden. [*William Nathaniel Brooker, 42 Malden Rd.*]

A procession was then formed, which made its way from the Council Offices via Duke's avenue to the Beverley Park. The band led, and following them came the 1st Malden troop of Boy Scouts, the Church Lads Brigade, and then the day school and Sunday school children marching four abreast.

On arrival at the Beverley Park which was beautifully decorated, the band proceeded to the bandstand, well appointed and under cover. The sports were then proceeded with. A heavy rainstorm about 3pm caused apprehension, but happily it was only of short duration and the sun was shining when the children assembled for their tea.

Many of the firemen were wearing ribbons for medals that had been distributed by Mrs Mursell, awarded for ten years service and over. The recipients were Second Officer Cullerne, Engineer V. Davison, Second Engineer Jennings, Firemen White, Burton, Willard, Baldwin, Brooks, Ayris and Captain Kirk.

Thursday's Bonfire

Although the New Malden celebrations were fixed to take place yesterday, Thursday, the actual Coronation day, was not allowed to pass by unrecognised. In the evening, a very large crowd, one of the largest that has ever been seen in Beverley Park assembled to witness a torchlight procession by the 1st Malden Troop of Boy Scouts. A large bonfire was lighted by Miss Kathleen Mursell, daughter of the Chairman of the Council. A large crowd remained till the bonfire burned out and also were entertained by watching the reflections of other bonfires in the surrounding districts.

For those who were unfortunate enough to be between the ages of 15 and 60 there was also an excellent programme of sports, including a tug-of-war, in which firemen, railwaymen, dairymen and postmen competed, a mile and two miles cycling race, while in a further portion of the field roundabouts and other side shows did a big business.

A concert followed the successful old people's tea at Burlington Road Schools, during which tobacco was distributed to the men, and tea in Coronation tins to the women.

At dusk the bandstand was illuminated and a large number of couples availed themselves of the opportunity afforded to dance in a marquee, whilst many more found pleasure in looking on at the more athletically inclined.'

Coronation Celebration New Malden June 23rd 1911. No.30(*Publ: Hide & Co. N.M. Real Photo. Postally unused*)

Malden's Charter Celebrations

Wednesday 23rd September 1936 was a very important date in Malden and Coombe's history. On that day, amidst great pageantry and celebration, the Charter of Incorporation was presented by the Lord Mayor of London to the town's Charter Mayor, creating the Borough of Malden and Coombe. Prior to 1936, the town's status had been the 'Urban District of The Maldens and Coombe'.

Before a town could become a Municipal Borough (i.e. a town with its own Town Council, Mayor and Chairman) it had to obtain a Royal Charter giving it the right to manage its affairs — a custom dating back many hundreds of years. In the early days, a chartered borough was a very important place indeed, and its status was a very highly valued privilege. Only a *Freeman* of the town could set up in business there, and it was difficult for outsiders to become *Freemen*.

To return to more modern times, and various snippets from the comprehensive reports in the *Surrey Comet* of the extensive ceremonial — and the Charter celebrations which lasted for several days:

Procession

The Great Day Begins

'Days of preparation had built up a great feeling of civic pride among old and young, and everybody was eagerly astir early on Wednesday.

"I was born and bred in Malden and I have never seen anything like it here before," was the comment of an old Malden resident and his remark sums up the general feeling.

Many people saw the Charter Mayoral procession leave the Council Offices and others were assembling in advantageous positions. At the district boundary in Burlington road where the Lord Mayor and his Sheriffs and officers were met, there was an enormous crowd. An awning was erected outside the Decca Record Company's works for the introductions.

Fog which had covered the district in the early morning gradually lifted, and had almost cleared by the time the Lord Mayor reached the boundary and the sun was struggling to break through. Vantage points for sightseers were the Beverley Brook bridge parapets where people were perched to look over the heads of the crowd below. Employees also crowded on to the roof of the Decca Record Co.'s works.'

(To the sound of peals of bells from Civic centres, six carriages had departed from the Municipal Offices via Malden Road, Malden Cross Roads, and Malden Way (Kingston by-pass) for the arrival at the District Boundary at 11.00am of The Lord Mayor of London and the Lady Mayoress in their ceremonial coach [see below] and accompanying State carriages)

Malden's Charter Celebrations 23.9.36. No.1   *(Publ: possibly Hide & Co. N.M. Real Photo. Postally unused.)*

Malden's Charter Celebrations 23.9 36.   1

Malden's Charter Celebrations 23.9.36. No.11   *(Publ: possibly Hide & Co. N.M. Real Photo. Postally unused)*
'Immediately before the Lord Mayor arrived there occurred one of those incidents which a waiting crowd so much enjoys. A hundred yards in front of the procession came a ramshackle rag-and-bone cart. A great cheer went up, but the driver kept a set face and drove on unperturbed.

After the introductions, which were made beneath the awning [*see page 53*], the two processions joined and proceeded, headed by the band of the Caterham branch of the British Legion, along Burlington road and Malden road to the Council Offices. The two roads were lined with cheering people, and flags and coloured streamers were everywhere. Malden cross roads were thronged, and outside the Council Offices was one of the biggest crowds ever seen there.' [*The above postcard shows part of that crowd — in the background is Cambridge Road with Tudor Williams' store to the left.* **Below**: A smaller crowd surveys the March '91 fire damage to the old Council Building and shops]

Malden's Charter Celebrations 23.9.36 No.10 *(Publ: possibly Hide & Co. N.M. Real Photo. Postally unused)*

Reception

'The formal reception and welcome of the Lord Mayor at the Council Offices was a colourful ceremony.

In the forecourt of the council offices a dais, covered in blue and gold, had been erected for the principals of the ceremony and on either side, in special enclosures, sat the distinguished guests. In the roadway, kept clear by mounted police, stood the guard of honour, provided by the 6th Battalion, the East Surrey Regiment (T.A.), and members of the Maldens and Coombe branch of the British Legion.

Eleven Visiting Mayors

Early arrivals in the enclosures were the mayors of neighbouring boroughs including those of Kingston, Surbiton, Wimbledon, Wandsworth, Reigate, Guildford, Sutton and Cheam, Richmond, Barnes, Mitcham and Godalming.

Heralded by cheers and a peal of bells the procession, now ten minutes behind schedule, was in sight. As it drew near a fireman, standing on the roof of the council offices, unfurled the new flag of the borough for the first time, alongside the Union Jack.'

[Then followed an inspection of the guard of honour, wreath-laying at the war memorial, a speech of welcome to the Lord Mayor and more formalities inside the council chamber.]

By 12.00 noon the procession to Beverley Park via Malden Road, King's Avenue, Howard Road, Duke's Avenue and Park View, was ready to depart for the formal presentation there of Malden's Charter of Incorporation. Bringing up the rear of the procession was the ubiquitous Borough Fire Brigade!

Massed crowds of mainly women and children lined the route and half an hour was allowed in the programming for the procession to reach the park where, following tree-planting ceremonies, the two Mayors proceeded to inspect massed formations of 3,500 school children from the borough's schools, as well as Boy Scouts, Girl Guides and other Junior Organisations.

The presentation by Sir Percy Vincent to the Charter Mayor, Major John Hill O.B.E. M.A., of the Charter of Incorporation took place at 12.45 pm, followed by speeches, a fanfare, and a Dedicatory Service conducted by The Right Reverend the Lord Bishop of Southwark.

By 1.15 pm, following musical interludes and the National Anthem, the procession re-formed for the return journey via King's Avenue to the 'State Banquet Hall' [a huge marquee decorated in the style of a banqueting hall at the Malden and Coombe sports ground] where a Civic Luncheon had been arranged for the VIP's and many guests. Meanwhile a free lunch box was distributed to every school child in Beverley Park.

[After these proceedings, the Lord Mayor and Lady Mayoress were escorted to the Borough boundary at Kingston Vale — and the residents of the new Borough were left to continue with their celebrations long into the night and following days:]

'A huge fun-fair took up a large part of Beverley Park; bands played popular music, and there were various displays of dancing during the afternoon. There was even a lifeboat available for inspection at which long queues formed.

At night the park was a blaze of light, and the glow in the sky could be seen for miles. Searchlights manned by the 316th (Surrey) Anti-Aircraft Company R.E., searched the clouds and after the grand fireworks display, a searchlight was trained on the lifeboat. Large audiences filled separate marquees twice nightly on Wednesday, Thursday and Friday for dancing, and for popular Variety concerts given by local entertainers.

On Thursday afternoon over 1,500 school children in the district competed in the sports held at Beverley Park, and that evening over 300 people attended the Charter Ball at the Malden and Coombe sports ground, where a temporary ballroom, with a parquet floor, reception and withdrawing rooms, and a large buffet hall had been erected.

Other events included entertainments for War Disabled and old folks. Free concerts, suppers and tickets for the local Plaza cinema ensured all sections of the community were able to enjoy themselves.'

Footnote:
[Surbiton also became a borough in 1936, and to put these local Charters into an historical perspective, some more dates for Surrey locations are given: Kingston (Royal Borough) — 1200; Guildford — 1257; Richmond — 1890; Wimbledon — 1905; Sutton and Cheam — 1934; Epsom and Ewell — 1937.

Administratively, the creation of The Greater London Council in 1965 absorbed north-east Surrey and the county borough of Croydon, as 'London's' boundary marched south. The urban districts of Carshalton, Mitcham and Morden, Coulsdon and Purley have also been lost to London.]

In the picture below, the new Methodist church which had been built in 1932, can be seen to the left of the tree. The bunting and flags decorating Malden Road would be there for probably one of three later events: 1935 was the 25th anniversary of King George V's accession to the throne, and the town might be celebrating that Silver Jubilee. Or this is another scene of Malden's Charter decorations. Alternatively, this could be 1937, when George VI had his coronation. On the corner of King's Avenue where the National Westminster Bank now stands, are the premises of W.H.Bird who sold second-hand furniture and floor coverings. Mr Bird lived in King's Avenue, just up the road from his shop. He was also a volunteer fireman, and when an emergency occurred and he was required to turn out with the brigade, a loud bell would sound in his house to alert him.

Decorations — Malden Road   (*Publ: Anon. possibly Hide & Co. N.M.Real Photo. Postally unused. Circa 1935/6*)

Shopfronts — Malden Road   *(Publ: Anon. Probably Hide & Co. N.M. Real Photo. Postally unused. c.1935-7)*
Malden Road decorated for either the King's Silver Jubilee of 1935, Malden's Charter celebrations 1936, or for
GeorgeVI's coronation 1937. The shopfronts shown which help to confirm the dates are [*left to right*] **No.21**: Ralph
Vanner, *Furniture dealer*; **No.19**: *Malden Cafe*, Mrs A.E.Woods; **No.17**: Hide & Co., *Photographers*; **No.15**: Hammett
Bros., *Butchers*; **No.13**: Home & Colonial Stores, *Provisions*; **No.11**: John Jameson, *Greengrocer*; **No.9**: *Beulah
Laundry*, T.W. Burkitt (receiving officer); **No.7**: Hawes & Co., *Auctioneers etc.,* **No.3/5** Alfred Jay, *Hosier/Outfitter*;
No.3: Gilbert H. Lutman, *Cars for Hire*; **No.1**: *Malden Tavern*, Charles E. Withers.   Hide & Co.'s photographic
business was started in 1876 by William Hide. It is still listed in a directory for 1940, but by 1948 the premises were
run by Davis & Davis Ltd., *Photographic Mat'l Dealers*. [*More information under Publishers* : W. Hide & Co. *page 6*]
Below: Today's view taken from a wider angle than the original scene, includes the old signal box and two flags.

(Publ: Hide & Co. N.M. Real Photo. Postally unused)

Mother's Union Garden Party The Vicarage June 15th 1914

SPORT &

SOCIAL

Malden Wanderers Cricket Team   (*Publ: probably Hide & Co. N.M. Real Photo. Postally unused. c.1914*)

The team photograph shown above is believed to be circa 1914. Unfortunately, none of the members of that team have been identified.

Prior to their first friendly match of the 1991 cricket season, a Malden Wanderer's XI kindly recreated to-day's team photograph at their ground in Cambridge Avenue.

Standing — *left to right*: A. Guest. P. Robinson. D. Samuel. A. Samuel. M. Hammerton. R. Hones. B. Ferris. (*umpire*)

Seated — *left to right*: B. Walters. D. Gale. D. Pauline. S. Fearnley. M. Mason.

N.A.A.S. Sports Meeting *(Publ: Hayden Studio, 135a Stroud Green Road, N.4. Real Photo. Postally unused. c.1921)*
This unused card has the above caption handwritten on the back, together with *Pearl sports ground, Norbiton. 1921.*
If this is correct, history has come full circle. Street directories for the early 1920's do list the Pearl Assurance
Athletic and Tennis Club, along with the London Irish Rugby Club and Sports and Football Grounds on the *site*
of the new Kingsmeadow Stadium, which is just inside the old borough of Malden And Coombe boundary. Old
maps also show what could be a stand of some sort marked on that site. *Old Kingstonians* Football Club also started
life there; they later merged with another local team to become *Kingstonian* Football Club at their ground in
Richmond Road, Kingston (now used for housing). In 1989 after 67 years there, the Club moved back to its
'original' home where a new stadium had also been completed for Kingston Athletic Club. The picture below, taken
during the Surrey County Championships on 21st April 1991, shows their modern stand in the background.

Flower Show New Malden July 17th 1912   *(Publ: Hide & Co. N.M.. Real Photo. Postally unused)*

Surrey Comet July 20th 1912

New Malden Flower Show.
Judges' Favourable Comments on the
Many Exhibits.

Host of Attractions

'The 14th annual exhibition in connection with the Maldens, Coombe, and Worcester Park Horticultural and Cottage Garden Society was held, by kind permission of Mr Ward E. Pearson, in the large meadow in Coombe Road, at the rear of Coombe House on Wednesday afternoon. (*see also pp.74-76*) Favoured with splendid weather which brought the inhabitants of the district flocking to the show in hundreds, the exhibition proved an undoubted success. The attractions for visitors and competitors were exceedingly numerous, and the various side shows including the familiar but never old-fashioned roundabouts, swings, cocoanut shies and shooting galleries found many patrons.

But of course the primary object of most of the numerous assembly of visitors was to view the many beautiful floral exhibits con

tained in two large marquees erected for the occasion.
(Then follows details and descriptions of produce on show, and a list of the judges names.)

The Luncheon

The luncheon was held at the Royal Oak hotel, Mr A.H.Smith making a genial chairman. After an enjoyable repast, which was well served by the proprietors, Mr Smith proposed the loyal toast.
(The judges were then toasted and thanked and they went on to pass general comments on excellence of the show and the produce.)

Attractions of the Fete

During the afternoon and evening enjoyable musical selections were given by the Maldens and Coombe military band, Mr A. Timbers conducting.

A number of pupils from Malden College gave a highly creditable display of physical exercises.   [*continued next page*]

Horse Parade Class 1. Market Place New Malden. *(Publ: Hide & Co. N.M. Real Photo. Postally unused. c.1912)*

Next followed a competitive horse parade in two classes. In class 1 — open to heavy draught horses in harness, without vehicles. (Winner: U.D.C. - driver Willard.)

In class 2 — for light harness horses with tradesmen's vehicles. (Winner: Coleman & Son, Dairyman - driver Higgins)

The parade had assembled at the Council Offices previous to the entry into the field.
(A list of Officials, Marshals, Judges then follows)

Horse Parade Class 1. Market Place New Malden. *(Publ: Hide & Co. N.M. Real Photo. Postally unused. c.1912)*

Horse Parade Class 2. Market Place New Malden   *(Publ: Hide & Co. N.M. Real Photo. Postally unused. c.1912)*

Following the parade came the athletic sports in which great enthusiasm was shown by the competitors, the officials and public alike. Events included running races for men, boys and girls, skipping races, long and high jumps, throwing the cricket ball and other equally interesting competitions.

Later in the day a display by the Fire Brigade was given under the direction of Captain C.J.Kirk. The programme included exhibition of steamer and escape drill, and proved of absorbing interest.

Other attractions included tug-of- war in which members of the Society, amateur gardeners, professional gardeners and cottagers participated.

Professor Douglas' royal Punch and Judy show with dog Toby, which is ever attractive to young and old alike, drew forth the usual hearty merriment from the numerous spectators of the misfortunes of Mr Punch.

Dancing in the reserved enclosure during the evening, and end of day fireworks display concluded the event.'*(Then follows over 1 newspaper column of show prizewinners.)*

Surrey Comet report of 15th Annual Flower Show on July 16th 1913:

The report again mentions the Malden and Coombe Military Band under Bandmaster A. Timbers being present, together with record crowds at the large meadow at the rear of Coombe House courtesy of Mr Ward E. Pearson. Besides the usual marquees displaying produce, and the luncheon report, the *Comet* reported that 'a short programme

[continued next page.....]

Flower Show New Malden July 16th 1913. No.8   *(Publ: Hide & Co. N.M. Real Photo. Postally used 1913)*

of sports was run off, and two popular entertainments were given by the Sunshines Pierrot troupe, [*see picture below*] consisting of Miss Connie Moore (Soprano), Miss Felicia Firmin (Soubrette and dancer), Mr Phil. Lester and Mr Jack Baxter (comedians), Mr A. Wallace (Baritone), Mr Austin Quifae (tenor) and Mr Arthur Bracewell (pianist) assisted by Messrs Wilkin and McGowan's marionettes.'

Flower Show New Malden July 16th 1913. No.1   *(Publ: Hide & Co. N.M. Real Photo. Postally used 1913)*

Church Parade New Malden 28.6.14 No. 4. *(Publ: Hide & Co. New Malden. Real Photo. Postally unused.)*
In 1896, ten years after the town's voluntary fire service had been formed, the firemen held their first "Church Parade", a charity fundraising event supported mainly by Temperance Societies and local Trades Union branches. It was to become an annual event, and this postcard, and those on following pages dated between 1911 and 1914, illustrate what the *Surrey Comet* report for the 1914 event refers to as the 'Friendly Societies Parade'. The fire of March 1991, which did millions of pounds worth of damage to the new shopping precinct on the site of the old fire station, ironically afforded the opportunity to take comparative pictures of modern fire engines in the High Street, but sadly in a working environment. The newspaper report of July 4th 1914 is reproduced in continuity on the next three pages with I think, appropriate illustrations. Note that the horse-drawn 'steamer' fire appliance was still in use, even though it was at about this time that fire brigades were changing to motorised appliances.[*see pp. 35-36*]

Church Parade New Malden 28.6.14 No 1.   *(Publ: Hide & Co. New Malden. Real Photo. Postally used 1914)*

FRIENDLY SOCIETIES' PARADE

"The sun shone brilliantly and continuously on the streets of New Malden on Sunday afternoon looking down on a procession of men working hard for a charitable object. The men were members of the procession formed in connection with the annual church parade and street collection of the local Friendly Societies and Men's Brotherhood organised on behalf of the Friendly Societies Convalescent Homes and the Fire Brigade Unions fund for widows and orphans. The procession, which paraded the whole of the district, was headed by the Malden Prize Band, the 1st Malden Boy Scouts (under Scoutmaster Odom) with their drum and fife band, and the Westbourne Park drum and fife band under Bandmaster Hobbs. In the procession there were fire engines from East Molesey, Metropolitan Water Board (Hampton Division), Esher and The Dittons, and Malden and Coombe, with 40 firemen

"Church Parade" New Malden June 8th 1913 No. 6 *(Publ: Hide & Co. New Malden. Real Photo. Postally used 1913)*
on foot from various brigades under Chief Officer Kirk. The Societies represented were Foresters, Oddfellows, Rechabites, Good Templars, National Deposit and Buffaloes, with members of the Men's Own Brotherhood, under Mr Mase, with their new banner. The officials for the procession were: Chief Marshal, Mr W. Sharman; Deputy Marshal, Mr W. Elliott; Side Marshals, Fireman Baldwin and Mr Beaumont; Honorary Secretary, Mr C.J.Hopper
Below:
The Parade passes between the Police Station, and the original fountain — sited opposite the Norbiton Park Hotel (later renamed The Fountain). The leading banner depicts 'Rev'd. Father Mathew'. Behind the second banner ('London Carmen's Trade Union, Wimbledon Branch No. 55') is a very leafy road — now the High Street.
Church Parade New Malden June 11th 1911   *(Publ: Hide & Co. New Malden. Real photo. Postally unused.)*

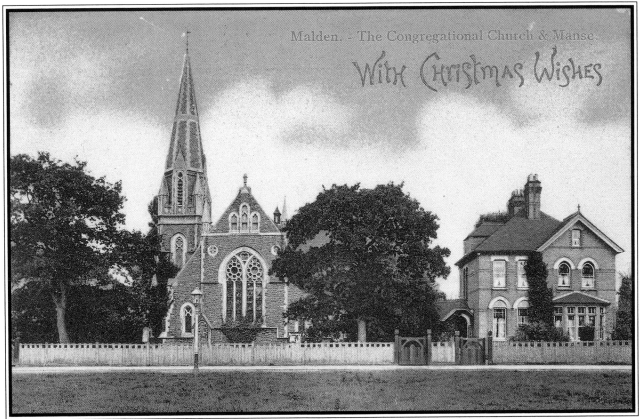

The Congregational Church & Manse. *(Publ:Collectors' Publ. Co. Colour litho print. Postally used Dec.25th 1908)*
At 3 o'clock the procession arrived at the New Malden Congregational Church, where a service was held in connection with the Brotherhood. Captain Kirk read the lessons, and the Brotherhood choir and orchestra gave selections. The street and church collections realised a total of £22-19-5d."

In the postcard view above, the house to the right is the Manse which had to be demolished in 1954, because of subsidence thought to have been caused by the earlier siting of a pond. For this reason it was not rebuilt, and a lawned garden now allows an attractive setting for wedding group photographs. The church, whose founders were the *Pascall* family (sweet manufacturers) and the Derry family (of London's drapers *Derry & Toms*), records its 110th anniversary this year. The entire roof was re-tiled in time for special celebrations from 19th/21st April.

Surrey Comet June 7th 1913 p.9

COUNCIL WORKMENS' OUTING

A Happy Day spent on Box Hill.

Councillor Hodgson's Generosity.

'On Saturday May 31st, a total of 83 people including Councillors, Departmental workmen and their wives departed in three charabancs from the Council Offices at 1pm. On arrival, luncheon was taken on the slopes of Box Hill. During the afternoon and evening not one slow moment was in evidence(!) The whole party was full of merriment and many went of to explore the locality. At 5pm at a different viewpoint, everyone re-assembled for tea. An impromptu sports event followed, in which the ladies also participated. Fortunately, there were no embarrassments by any of the party rolling down the slopes.'
[*Thanks having been expressed by the workmen and their wives to the organisers, were then reciprocated by the councillors for everyone's attendance, stating that they hoped this would become an annual event* because of the obvious success of the day.*]

'The return journey commenced at 7pm, and great merriment was experienced by the occasional dips along the hilly roads coupled up with several arranged explosions of loud laughter.'
Arrival back at the Council Offices seems to have been a noisy affair with much cheering and handshaking.

*On Saturday June 13th 1914, a similar event took place. This time the *Surrey Comet* reported that 'a party numbering 124 departed at noon for luncheon on Box Hill, several of the Surrey beauty spots being visited by charabanc during the afternoon.'

It is likely that what was to become an annual event, would have been suspended during the years of the first World War.

A limiting factor in planning any distant outing by charabanc in those days, was the vehicle's *top* speed of 12 m.p.h.

"Council Outing" New Malden May 31st 1913   *(Publ: Hide & Co. N.M. Real Photo. Postally used 1913)*

Coombe Lane. Coombe *(Publ: T.Thomas, The library, N.M..No131764. Colour litho print. Postally unused)*
The precise location of this postcard view of circa 1910 has not been established

COOMBE

Coombe House — A photograph from the Kingston Heritage Centre collection.

In 1908 and 1909 the local Flower Shows were both held on a Wednesday. The venue in each case was the 'lower meadows of **Coombe House**' — a 1750's building which had been in its time a boy's boarding school and a sanatorium, until 1867 when it became privately owned again. In 1888, it still had many outbuildings (stable blocks, coach-house, laundry block, carriage shed, and to-day's two remaining gate lodges). Demolished during the 1930's, it stood at the top of Trap's Lane [*see p.77*]. The *Surrey Comet* of *24th July 1909* after the usual, comprehensive report of the organisation, luncheon and prizewinners, has several paragraphs given to the day's amusements and, lower down the same page, a report of the following day's Sunday School Treat at the same location.

The Amusements.

'In addition to the attractions of the exhibits and the fair there were various competitions, amusements and other displays. A display was to have been given on behalf of the Surrey Beekeepers' Association by the secretary, Mr. F.B.White, but this was unavoidably cancelled.

Much interest was taken in a procession of decorated cycles and mailcarts, and the entrants had very prettily decorated their machines. The judge was Mrs Hodgson.

A shooting competition was in progress from 3 p.m. till dusk, and there were fairly large entries for this event. Two al fresco concerts were given during the afternoon. After the prize distribution the London Division of the Royal Naval Volunteer Reserve gave a display, by permission of Commander the Hon. Rupert Guinness, with a 12 pounder field gun. There were also sabre and bayonet contests and blindfold boxing bouts; while C.P.O. Bremner R.M.A., the Navy champion, gave an astonishing exhibition of axe swinging. At the conclusion the volunteers were thanked and complimented by Mrs Currie for their work. The 1st Malden troop of Boy Scouts, including the patrols, with the "Wolves" and the "Kangaroos", under Scoutmaster W. Odom, gave an illustration of their activities, which was watched with keen interest by a large number of those present. Tugs-of-war were also a feature, contests taking place between members of the society, amateurs, gardeners and cottagers, policemen and tramwaymen, and firemen and railwaymen. A tent was set aside for the Malden Nursing Institute, where a number of friends and nurses of that body sold flowers and refreshments in aid of the funds. Dancing was carried on at night in a special enclosure, under the direction of Messrs F. Slaughter and G.W.Pearce, who acted as M.C.'s. The concluding feature was a display of fire-works, through the kindness of Mr P.G.W. Typke, by Messrs Joseph Wells and Co. The band of the 2nd City of London Royal Fusiliers played a selection of music during the afternoon under the baton of Mr John Whates. Refreshments were provided by Mr C.E. Lemon of Teddington.

The prizes were distributed by Mrs Laurence Currie, who was heartily thanked for so doing and for acting as judge for the ladies' classes.'

And in another report from the same page:

SUNDAY SCHOOL TREAT. - 'The scholars attending the New Malden Sunday Schools connected with the Parish Church had their annual treat in the grounds below Coombe House, by permission of Dr. Pearson*, on Thursday afternoon. Vans were kindly lent by various tradesmen to convey the smaller children to the field, the others assembling in Lime Grove and walking from there to the meadow. Many of the mechanical amusements utilised at the previous day's flower show were left standing, and were largely patronised by the children. About 550 youngsters were present with the teachers, and during the evening many of the parents arrived. Tea was served at 4.30 by Mr Smith, who had charge of the catering. During the afternoon and evening various races were enjoyed by the children, and cricket and other sports were indulged in. In the absence of the Rev. J.T. Poole, Mr W.J. Cole superintended the arrangements for the boys. Later in the evening the prizes were presented.'

*Surrey Comet May 15th 1915:

Dr. Frederick Stark Pearson D.Sc. of Coombe House was reported as a victim of the German torpedoing of the Lusitania. Having lived at Coombe House for about 6 years, he was travelling back from a month's trip to the United States with his wife who, it was assumed in the report, had also perished at sea.

Uncaptioned Fairground Scene   *(Publ: possibly Hide & Co. N.M. Real Photo. Postally unused. c.1908/9)*

Coombe & Malden Flower Show. July 22nd 1908.   *(Publ: probably Hide & Co. N.M. Real Photo. Postally unused)*

The publisher captioned these postcards "Coombe & Malden Flower Show", but the *Surrey Comet* reported them as the "Malden & Coombe Flower Show and Fete". Whatever they were called or whenever they were held, it is clear from all the organised entertainment and attractions, that they were one of *the* social occasions every year in the area.   Although the post cards of these events still turn up, I have yet to find one which shows any of the displays of flowers or fruit and vegetables! (Perhaps the light inside the marquees was not all it could have been for photography?) In both pictures almost everyone is wearing a hat of some sort, the Edwardian styles typified by the ladies with flowery broad brims, and the gents with their straw boaters.

Coombe & Malden Flower Show. July 21st 1909.   *(Publ: probably Hide & Co. N.M. Real Photo. Postally unused)*

Coombe Hill   *(Publ: Anon. possibly Hide & Co. N.M. Real Photo. Postally used 1912)*

The caption on this card is quite misleading to a local historian. (A New Malden nonogenarian was able to point me in the right direction!) It is of course the top of Traps Lane, at the junction with Coombe Lane West and the slip road forming a small triangle of land there. Old maps have always shown this to be named 'Traps Lane' after *Madam Trap,* an occupier of a nearby house and garden whose precise location remains a mystery to this day. Perhaps the publisher captioned it *Coombe Hill* because this was a locally accepted name for the same area. The old maps also showed a track across the triangle itself, indicated above by the barrier/gate behind the two men. Out of picture left was Coombe House and grounds, [*see p.74*] of which only two gate lodges remain — one at this point, at the entrance to Fitzgeorge Avenue, — the other almost opposite the entrance to Warren Road, Coombe Lane.

Warren Road. New Malden   *(Publ: Anon. Sepia litho print. Perf. left edge. Postally unused. Circa 1920's)*

Behind the gated entrance to Warren Road lie not only exclusive addresses, golf courses and mansions set in beautiful estates, but a story of *rights of way* and the rights of ordinary people. In the year that Queen Victoria came to the throne, the Duke of Cambridge purchased the entire Coombe Estate, including *The Warren* as it was then known. The Duke had signs erected denying all access to what had been — for as far back as anyone could remember — land used by all sections of the community for recreational pursuits, and through which an ancient track was used as a direct route by pedestrians, horse-powered carts, and even horse fanciers going to Epsom races. Immediate protests resulted only in several years concessionary use of the track until 1850, when the Duke reinforced his claim by posting a guard at ornamental gates set across the entrance. The 2nd Duke inherited the Estate, and the problem, when his father died shortly after this, and firmly pursued his father's policy of allowing

ENTRANCE TO WARREN ROAD, COOMBE END.

Entrance to Warren Road — Coombe end.*(Publ: Balmer, Kingston. Sepia litho print. Postally unused. Circa 1920's)*
only "respectable" people through. Local feelings on the matter were polarised between those who saw a royal
Duke and benefactor being unnecessarily humiliated — and those who raised £200 by a public fund to take the
Duke to court at Croydon Assizes in 1853. Despite a "special jury of Gentlemen" chosen for the hearing, a
procession of witnesses from all walks of life (but especially those able to state what an early map clearly showed
— that *The Warren* was, and always had been a public thoroughfare), caused the judge to call a halt to the
proceedings. The "special jury" found in favour of the public in its unrestricted use of *The Warren* as *a footpath only*.
The enraged Duke had to pay all the costs of 'The Battle of Coombe Warren' as *The Times* called it. Great celebrations
ensued as huge crowds met the returning heroes at the gate on Kingston Hill to ceremoniously remove the lock.
Below: Today, Warren Road has a guarded, rising barrier (out of view) to control *traffic* entering at certain times.

Selected Bibliography

TITLE	AUTHOR	PUBLISHER
Surrey Past and Present	Edited by F.E. Manning M.A.	S.E.R.A. 1971
Local History Research and Writing	David Iredale	Elmfield Press 1974 ISBN 0 7057 0041 0
The Place Names of Surrey	Mawer, Stenton, Bonner, Gover	Cambridge University Press. 1969
A History of Malden	Kenneth N. Ross	1947
Half a Century of Kingston History	F.S. Merryweather	1887 — since reprinted (1976)
Kingston upon Thames — a dictionary of local history	G.B. Greenwood	Martin & Greenwood
The History of Malden Parochial School 1864-1964	F.E. Harman	—
Old Malden, Worcester Park and District	H.V. Molesworth-Roberts	—
The Manor of Coombe or Coombe Neville	L.E. Gent	Occasional Paper No.3 K.U.T.A.S. 1979
All Change	June Sampson	St. Luke's Church, Kingston
Kingston Then and Now	Margaret Bellars	Michael Lancet
Eighty Years ago and Yesterday — Memories of Malden	Margery Weekes	(Published privately) 1990
MALDEN — Old & New A Pictorial History	Stephen H. Day	Marine Day Publishers 1990
Picture Postcards of the Golden Age—A Collector's Guide	Tonie & Valmai Holt	McGibbon & Kee
Picture Postcards and their Publishers	Antony Byatt	Golden Age Postcard Books 1978
Postcard Collecting — — a beginner's guide	Brian Lund	Reflections of a Bygone Age. Keyworth, Notts.
'Early Views of New Malden' 18 photos. + notes	Kingston Heritage (A4 folder)	Royal Borough of Kingston upon Thames
Kingston in Maps — Archive Teaching Unit 4	Kingston Heritage (A3 folder)	Royal Borough of Kingston upon Thames
Directories — guides to local history sources No.1	Rita J. Ensing	Wandsworth Historical Society
Street Directories for Kingston and District	— —	Kelly's & Phillipson's
The Surrey Comet 1896 - 1936		